I Am Not Your Average Black Woman

by

Shakirah "O"mazing

TABLE OF CONTENTS

DEDICATION

Life is so unexpected. Life has no reset button, or do over.

But, I disagree.

Life is what you are willing to accept and move from that purpose.

For example, we cannot predict other people's behavior or actions.

Unfortunately, people cannot be controlled.

What can be controlled is our own emotions, reactions and thoughts.

We each go through trials harder than some and oftentimes wonder
why?

I learn to accept that my pain is a part of my purpose.

It sounds bizarre but everything has a divine reason.

My Creator makes no mistakes and He already knows how our story
will project.

The issue is we as humans never go with the flow and God knows that.

As this book was written, my pain never stopped.

My mentality did not magically create wonderful and positive things.

Life is not magical but you can create your own magic.

This collection of poetry is for the unpredictable, painful and joyous
era we live in.

The uncertainty, the doubts, the fears, the unknown and even the
prejudice, is a part of life.

How we choose to adapt to the obstacles is on us..........

I Am Not Your Average Black Woman,Part I.

By Shakirah "O"mazing.

To Our Youth

We must educate our youth to become great; challenge them and not to give up. Society portrays our youth, especially blacks as criminals and statistics. We must break this cycle of negative thinking and hatred that has plagued the black race for too many years. It starts with our youth.

We must uplift, empower, and educate them to reach their highest potential in life. We must never let society take their minds and rob our youth of their entitlement to freedom of speech and freedom to be different.

So, I say this to all our youth---Dream, never give up, and be proud of who you are.

CONSPIRACY

I have situations on my mind that are puzzling.

Is it unrealistic to want a happy life despite constant fights?

Perhaps I overthink and expect too much.

I must learn to better adapt.

The conspiracy is that I create my own storms because deep down inside, I accept it as a norm.

I grew up accepting confusion, concluding I could never escape the pressures of my mind.

In all reality, I have become my own enemy.

I must knock down my own drama accordingly.

I will not be a victim of circumstances.

I have better chances of surviving my own lunacy.

Surprisingly, those with the most troubled past endure it all through time.

MOVE WITH A PURPOSE

When you enter a room, let their stares motivate you.

Let them motivate you to never become afraid of the unknown.

Let the stares challenge you to the point you move fearlessly.

Anytime you walk, leave them with anxiousness.

Your purpose is to move with a purpose.

Never worry about anyone else's insecurities.

In all actuality, your mentality must be strong.

You are like the lion in the jungle and you are always ready to rumble.

SUICIDE

Thoughts of emptiness, regret and what ifs enter my mind.

Feelings of defeat, anger and feeling like the world around me is crashing and burning.

No one seems to understand my pain.

No one cares that I have thoughts of running away.

No one thinks to ask me how I am doing when I am constantly reviewing the negativity in my head that is constantly brewing.

I do not want to feel alone.

I do not want to feel hurt.

I do not want to feel like drowning in my own misery and those who surround me are obsolete.

I just ask for relief.

I just ask for sympathy.

I just ask for this thing called suicide not to destroy my mind.

In the meantime, I will have no choice but to overcome the troubles that keep me in a huddle.

The chains will break off me, and there will be no more struggles.

For anyone having a hard time coping with this, please seek help because life is meant to be enjoyed.

You are never alone. You will get through the pain, and storms never last too long.

POETIC JUSTICE

I put the pen to my paper and write my thoughts as they come to me.

I want to inspire groups of people who feel out of touch.

In this world, people are filled with ideas of themselves that they will never be able to prevail.

Many people think they are designed to fail.

I use my poems to provoke deep and profound thoughts.

What is justice if people cannot heal what is broken?

My poems are poetic.

There are forces that drive me from within.

I want my words to give hope.

I have a presence so deep that it's unforgettable.

CRASHING DOWN!

Worry.

Worrying causes me to crash down.

Anxiety.

Anxiety causes me to crash down.

Insanity.

Can I really claim I might be insane from political rants to stressful times?

Uncertainty is at an all-time high.

I know I am supposed to use my inner strengths to make me wiser and sufficient.

Mentally, I need to break away from the insanity, anxiety, and uncertainty.

I just pray one day to keep it all together for my sake.

LET ME WALK THROUGH

No weapon formed against me shall prosper; therefore, let me walk through that crowd.

Let me slide through like a snake.

No turbulence or disruption can stop my progression.

Let me walk through like I told you, so I can clarify any misunderstanding you may have.

For instance, I can walk through any situation without a look of defeat for any doubts you may have.

My response is this: I keep my eyes up above, never lose my faith, and no matter what, this is what my Creator saith!

BLACK AND PROUD

Say it loud!

I am black, and I am proud like James Brown.

I have too much going on to let anyone block my way.

I will not let the world put me in disarray.

I need order and structure to flow my way.

I need stability that is clear to me.

My ancestors did not sacrifice for me not to speak and question the immoralities that are portrayed in our society.

Sometimes our actions can be used against us like a knife that cuts deep.

My blackness cannot be carved like a piece of cheese.

Please do not become afraid of my time to shine.

Like in *Black Panther*, I cannot be bound.

INCARCERATED

Ugly,

Demeaning,

Cruel.

Too many minorities are in the system.

There is so much despair.

Politicians want to see us fail.

The prison system is designed to make bail impossible.

It is a money-making business to no avail.

The system profits from you, family, and friends.

We all suffer from this within.

Damn.

Can we just try to overcome?

I am tired of seeing my young minorities try to survive in the wind.

It is becoming a vicious cycle that never seems to end.

We must educate ourselves on the broken system to really win.

YOUNG BLACK MAN

To my young, black man, I say unto you.

Please keep your hands up when the police approach you.

It is sad they will shoot you if you flinch or move.

I know it is sad that you must pick your battles when it involves your life, which matters.

On the news, they choose who they want to know the truth.

The truth is officers are quick to shoot an unarmed black man and report it as self-defense.

Listen to me. I am no fool.

By any means, I do not believe the young, black man is always a threat.

The officers are always scared, which is a straight fact.

Let us open our minds to the reality that race in America is always an issue.

Young, black man, I pray for you. You are my brother, cousin and husband too.

America, look what you've done.

It is time to help our youth and stop being uncouth.

It is time to stop killing our young, black men. It's not cool.

They will wipe all of them out and there will be no race.

Woman without the young, black man is a disgrace.

WHY?

Why does the government divide and try to alienate people?

Why do we not have affordable education to have more information to help better our situations?

Do they not want us to better our generation and become more knowledgeable about the nation?

Why do young black men in America become easily incarcerated, victims of isolation and deprivation?

Why does the deprivation, isolation, and incarceration belittle and demean the young black man's reputation?

Why are people in politics already rich?

Why are some politicians using their power to dominate, divide, and manipulate those who have no hope to rise above the stipulations that are put in place to cause fear and lack of communication?

Why are people sleeping in the streets, struggling to survive and wondering if they will be able to stay alive?

Why are people worried about paying their rent, putting food on the table, and still making it to their jobs that pay too little?

Why is it hard to survive in this world where the money you have is more important than the values and principles you carry?

Why do we live in a world where babies are being killed by their own parents who are expected to love, nurture, and heal?

Why are poor people looked over and ignored, while the rich are catered to? Being put on a pedestal. Why do people treat them greater than the Creator?

Why do some police officers gun down African American men but do not question the white supremacist?

Why do some people in power use and abuse the system, while those from the system are weakened and foolish?

Why is it easy to get arrested but hard to become employed?

My main question is this: Why do I have to pretend to be someone I am not for people to respect me, honor me, and listen to me?

Why do people not understand that I come from a life of pain and often, my behavior cannot be explained?

Why is there racism in America, when it is supposed to be a land of opportunity and equality?

Why are you not free?

TROUBLE

Trouble is around me all the time.

Trouble occupies my time, and it consumes my mind.

I am so mentally tired of the trouble. I need it to disappear like a bubble.

I need peace of mind.

I want to better define who I am.

I just need a better chance to enhance what is already inside of me.

Motivation and determination are made from my D.N.A.

No matter what trouble may come around me, I have the tools to maneuver.

I move with a purpose, and I will never allow defeat to wipe me off my feet.

DO WHAT YOU CAN FOR YOURSELF

I may not be able to see in the fog or through the smoke,

but I do see my confidence and courage.

I will use all those weapons that were used against me as tools to become efficient.

I never thought, for any second, I had lost my will to overcome the challenges.

I will rise and rise until I cannot.

Like baking bread, I will rise to the top and pop up like the strength I have from within.

THE ROAD TO SUCCESS

The bumps, hills, and rocks are in your way while you stumble to reach the top.

Knock over those rocks, walk up those hills, and jump over those bumps.

No one ever said the road to success was going to be a walk in the park.

You may get a little dirty, a little scratched, but you must keep going until the end.

You do not want any regrets or wonder about what-ifs in life.

So, you'll go down the unexpected, you will be surprised on the road to success what you will find: progress and faithfulness.

WHAT MORE CAN I SAY?

Great minds often lose sight and hope.

Great minds often become consumed with everyday anticipations and lose their concentration.

What more can I say about my mind?

My thoughts come tumbling down like an airplane crashing in the sky.

What more can I say when I cannot convince myself to seek professional help?

My mind is great. Yes, indeed.

But it can become so overcrowded with doubt and fear that I'll forget to think of my capabilities.

The truth of the matter is

I cannot afford to lose my grip.

I must keep focusing on my championships.

IT'S NOT OVER!

I know you are going through a situation, and it appears impossible to bear.

But I was taught never to move with fear.

You see, whatever the situation is, it does not define who you are.

In fact, it can motivate, cultivate, and elevate you into success.

It's not over until you choose to quit. Commit and get your mind intact.

Think about this: The greatest leader had to become their own cheerleader.

My Highest Power gave me the necessary brainpower to overcome and devour any challenges.

Like the lion chasing the deer, he moves with no fear!

THE SPECIAL ONE

I look at myself, and what do you think comes to my mind?

Courageous, motivated, and determined.

But I also see disappointment, regret, and pain.

Is it safe to say that, as human beings, we have different thoughts of how we see ourselves through others?

I have been feeling a way about myself for so long that I often must remember to embrace my flaws.

I am the special one who is never left alone or in a negative space.

I say this for a reason.

I am equipped with so many gifts that any negativity that comes near me will disappear like a thief in the night.

All my greatest memories will ignite.

INDEPENDENCE

Men say an independent woman is a gift.

I want women to see their independence as a mindset.

How many times have we as women had to downgrade our way of thinking to make a man feel secure?

Women let us keep it real.

Some men are insecure, and some women are not confident.

It appears that we women are looked upon as objects.

Independence is a gift.

Men and women should not be afraid to show their inner strength.

Let us live in a world where we are all self-sufficient.

An independent man is just as powerful.

To my men and to my women, let us all come together to show the world that we as a black race can conquer all and stand tall!

USED

I gave you all I could, but you were dissatisfied.

I made sure things were in order, but you were still unhappy on the inside.

So, I asked myself, "What should I do?"

Will I continue to be used, or will I use my strength to reproduce my confidence?

How long can I continue to allow verbal abuse?

How long until I realize I cannot satisfy everyone?

I will not be used and looked upon as a fool.

I am confident in who I am.

No matter who I am or who you think I am, I never allow what others think of me to move me.

Like a snake, I slide through the foolery.

THE URGE TO QUIT

I have too much to do.

Little time to do it.

And the urge to quit frequents my mind a million times.

I keep trying and trying until I can no longer try.

The urgency to be great never leaves my mind.

Whoever is reading this poem, I urge you to keep moving on.

Don't let wary thoughts consume your mind.

The urge to quit can make you stagnate.

I write what I feel to motivate those who need to be healed.

My destiny must be fulfilled.

I knock over struggles like Lego blocks; you move to crumble.

Like the big blue ox, I could never be put into a box.

The urge to quit does not coexist.

Let the fire inside you keep you alive!

LET ME THINK

Let me think of the many times I have cried and been tied down in other people's trials.

It appears my mind keeps jumping to the many denials.

Let me think. How many miles have I been running up and down, pretending to keep a smile on my face?

Damn.

How much disgrace has been interlaced, like a shoestring that could never stay straight?

Let me think ...

Do I need to take a couple sips of my drink, rethink, and then get in sync with myself?

Let me think ...

MY BLESSINGS FLOW

What I seek is what I receive.

Any blessing that comes my way, I will pick it up like money found on the ground.

I move to the side to collect my blessings over and over.

I do not use any genie in a bottle or special tricks.

My mind is my tool, and my faith is my escape.

My blessings flow like rain that tastes like champagne.

Let it pour, let it pour until there are no limits to reach anymore.

I Did Not Forget

I did not forget those who lied on me or never thought I could climb any wall that kept me from reaching my prime.

I did not forget the people who doubted me because those people made me a mastermind.

They made me want to figure out how to get to my success around the smoke and clouds.

In order to become great, I must learn to move and shake.

So, thank you to the haters who wished on a star that my charm and glamour would just wash away.

FAMILY

Fighting to stick together no matter what.

Accepting the flaws we have among each other.

Making sure no one is in trouble and looking out for each other.

In sync with each other and praying no one fails.

Loving each other despite the hard times.

Yielding protection and not worrying about a sense of direction.

I wish my family was more connected.

I AM LOVING WHO I AM!

To my ladies, self-love is the first love.

Respect is a two-way street.

Do not accept anything from a man that makes you second guess who you are.

I am loving who I am since I know my worth.

I am loving who I am since I know it helps me move forth.

To my ladies, be proud!

Speak up when you are tired of the lies, the deceit, and never look upon yourself as just a trick or treat.

It is not always easy being a woman, that I know.

But as time goes, you will truly learn that loving who you are takes time.

Just keep on climbing to reach those stars.

MY PAIN

Turn your pain into profit.

This is what I say to myself.

I have a story to tell that people should know either way.

I am not afraid of how people will look at me.

We all have a story to tell that speaks the truth.

I am not ashamed of what my past may portray.

I hold my head up high like I am in the mountains. I can almost touch the sky.

I will stay true to who I really am.

No one can judge me since we all have scars.

I just pray one day to tell my story to someone who will say, "You are an inspiration all the way!"

SHOUT!

I have been down so long that I cannot stay there.

I look to the sky, and I think of happy times.

I cry out and shout!

I will not stay down.

I must pick up the pace and keep winning the race.

Great people never sit down in disgrace.

They use the broken pieces as motivation to climb and stay on their grind.

Shout if you must that you will reach the top no matter what.

No matter how many times you may fall, even if you must crawl.

Keep going until you cannot.

There is always light at the end of the tunnel despite all the troubles.

It Will Get Better

When I walk out of my door, I have thoughts of a new day.

When I strut down the street, whatever was standing in my way cannot defeat me.

Whatever pain I face, I stare at it with strength and repeat, "I cannot stay down. I cannot stay down."

Does the lion give up when it loses its prey?

I hold my head high and brush off the worry and prepare myself for the victory.

It will fall in my lap, and once it does, no one can stop it.

It will get better if I just believe it!

THE CHASE

He has a look that most want.

He has the style that most cannot have.

He has a presence in a room full of peasants.

He talks with confidence, so when he speaks, you see his self-confidence.

He does not need to brag about his many ways.

He does not need to chase women when he moves at a steady pace.

His goal is to keep going with his life in a positive place.

He wants to be the man a real woman needs to embrace.

And whoever his woman is, she could never feel misplaced.

LESSONS

Heartbroken, yes.

Defeated, not yet.

Disappointed, of course.

Regretful, no.

I just wish I would have been more careful, that's all.

Foolish, indeed.

Angry, yeah, but not with anyone but myself.

I use my life lessons as a tool to teach me how to move correctly.

Any wrong move can have a major effect.

But I cannot obsess over my past.

I just look at the lessons as stepping stones and use them to surpass the difficulty.

I just go with the flow and whatever way it goes,

I use it to grow.

FIERCE AND FLAWLESS

The words that best describe me are fierce and flawless.

I walk down the street wearing nothing but confidence.

I am flawless in every motion.

I do not need to look to anyone else to validate me.

I do not let anyone's whispers about me puzzle me.

I let them keep talking while I am walking, and their whispers to me
sound like birds squawking.

Being flawless is natural for me because I am put together by grace
and mercy.

Those are the ingredients that make me a complete recipe.

I have no fears that I must worry about.

My fierceness stands out like a knight in the night, ready to protect and
fight.

Beyoncé said it best: "I woke up like this."

So, I say to myself, keep on going because I am highly blessed.

Being fierce and flawless does not come so easily.

But each day, I am wearing it so lovely.

CRY

Dry your eyes from lack of love.

Cry if it helps your soul.

Cry to release from the cold world.

Cry to anticipate a change that will soon come, so you can prevail.

Cry to release the negativity that hindered your creativity.

Crying does not make you weak.

No one will always have it all together, but you will get better over time.

Life is meant to be treasured.

So occasionally it is okay, just so your soul knows you are still alive!

BROKE

When I hear the word "broke," this is what comes to me: *No hope, no light.*

Some people are breaking in mind, spirit, and health and have no real sense of who to be or where to go.

I often find myself daydreaming.

I do not want a broken state of mind when I know I can be in my prime.

Broke is a state of mind, and no matter what, I cannot and will not choke.

I will get my time to shine.

I am not broke!

I am not broke!

I am rich in mind and spirit.

My flesh will not be weak.

I will go and reach my highest peak.

www.ingramcontent.com/pod-product-compliance
Lightning Source LLC
LaVergne TN
LVHW051819080426
835513LV00017B/2013